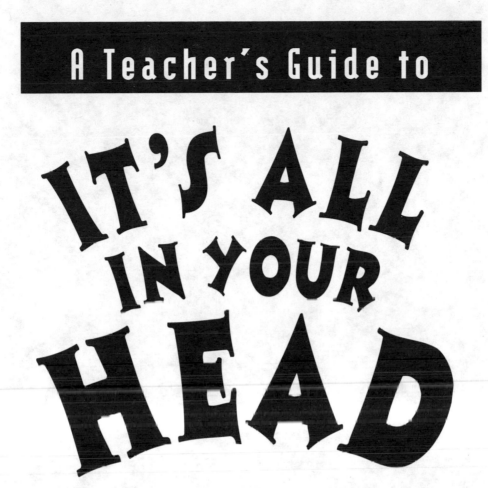

A Teacher's Guide to

IT'S ALL IN YOUR HEAD

SUSAN L. BARRETT

A Guide to Understanding Your Brain and Boosting Your Brain Power

free spirit
PUBLISHING®
Works for kids™

ISBN 0-915793-46-6

10 9 8 7 6
Printed in the United States of America

Edited by Pamela Espeland
Cover and book design by MacLean & Tuminelly

Free Spirit Publishing Inc.
400 First Avenue North, Suite 616
Minneapolis, MN 55401
(612) 338-2068

CONTENTS

INTRODUCTION

During the past 25 years, we have discovered more about the human brain than was ever thought possible. Many secrets have been revealed, but we still have a long way to go before we truly can understand this magnificent "mind machine."

How can we, as teachers, guide our students in exploring the knowns and unknowns about the human brain? What do kids really want to know about the brain? In what ways will learning more about the brain boost their brain power? Where can they search for information? How can they use what they learn in their everyday lives? What new adventures lie ahead in future brain research? As facilitators, how can we encourage students to get the most mileage out of their brains?

We may not find all of the answers in a short unit of study, or even in our lifetime, but what's most important is to persevere in our efforts to use *our* brain to study the brain. It's true: Our brain is the only organ that studies itself! It seems that the more we know, the more we want to know. As you and your students pursue some of the activities in this Teacher's Guide, you may come to a new awareness of your own tremendous potential and hidden personal abilities. You may even discover some things about your teaching and learning styles that you never recognized before.

This Teacher's Guide is designed to be used in conjunction with the student book, *It's All in Your Head: A Guide to Understanding Your Brain and Boosting Your Brain Power*. As a resource teacher who has been working with gifted students for over 12 years, I have successfully used these activities with my own students.

Most often, I have taught them in pull-out classes, but they may also be brought into the regular classroom setting. All kids are interested in the brain and how it works, not just gifted kids.

Studying the brain and how to boost its power can be considered an interdisciplinary topic, since several curriculum areas are integrated throughout the course of study. Or you might choose to use *It's All in Your Head* as a thematic teaching unit, expanding or altering particular areas according to your students' age level and learning needs and your own teaching style. In other words, this guide is meant to be *flexible*. You don't have to follow the parts in sequence, and you may use your own creativity to adapt the activities. Also, because no book on the brain can begin to exhaust this fascinating topic—and because new information about the brain seems to reveal itself annually, sometimes daily—you and your students will probably want to search these latest findings and stay up-to-date on what's going on in this exciting area.

This Teacher's Guide is divided into sections which relate directly to the chapters in the student book. A single section may cover several topics from that book. Please feel free to adjust the order and invent your own activities. If you teach *It's All in Your Head* as a unit, it will take from 6 to 12 weeks, depending on how often you meet with your students. Or you might choose to use parts of the book for enrichment activities or other specific purposes. For example, if your students are involved with a national inventing contest, you could cover the sections on creativity, problem-solving, and inventing.

Each section of this Teacher's Guide includes the following three elements:

1.   concepts (ideas your students will learn in that section),

2.   materials (resources and supplies you will need to teach that section), and

3.   student activities (discussion questions, experiments, hands-on ideas, demonstrations, etc.).

A list of resources, including written and audiovisual materials as well as hands-on models, is found on pages 41–43. You may want to send for some of these materials before you start teaching It's All in Your Head.

Since most students enjoy a good mystery, perhaps we can look at the study of the human brain as an experience in searching for clues which could lead us in exciting directions. As you and your students embark on your journey into understanding our complex "mind machine," you may find that some students are intrigued by a particular topic and would like to pursue it further. Encourage, guide, and support them in their efforts to discover new information and ideas. Perhaps they will choose to create a product or prepare a presentation to share their findings with the rest of the class. That's really what this Guide is all about: learning together and from each other.

As teachers, we owe it to ourselves and our students to increase our knowledge about how and why we think the way we do. If it's true that we use only 2-5 percent of our brain capacity, which current estimates indicate, then we need to keep searching for ways to tap into the other 95-98 percent. I hope that It's All in Your Head opens new doors for you and your students.

Susan L. Barrett
1992

THE AMAZING BRAIN

It's All in Your Head **pages 1–22**

Concept

Students will learn basic principles about the brain's physical structure and functions.

Materials

▶ Plastic or cardboard model of the human brain, such as "Anamodo" (see page 41)*

▶ Newsprint or other paper for brainstorming

▶ Box or other container big enough to hold the model

▶ Printed signs for simulation activity (see Activity #6, page 4)

▶ Green 3" x 5" index cards for Brain Trivia Game

▶ Sample Brain Trivia questions (see Activity #7, page 4)

▶ File box for Brain Trivia card storage

Activities

1. Introduce the unit.

Briefly describe some of the topics you and your students will be exploring together. For an at-a-glance outline, see the Contents for the student book.

2. Show a model of the human brain.

Have students brainstorm two lists: "What We Already Know about the Brain" and "What We Want to Learn about the Brain." Review and discuss their lists. Next, have them list everything their brain is doing right now, at this very moment. Share responses.

3. Explore the differences between the brain and mind.

Put the model of the brain inside a box or container. Ask, "Can the two terms 'brain' and 'mind' be used interchangeably? Why or why not?" Briefly discuss the *connectionists*— scientists who are attempting to link the brain's psychology and biology. Ask, "Will we ever develop a 'thinking machine' that mimics the human brain? Do you think a computer could ever do everything the brain does? Why or why not?"

4. Use the model to locate important parts of the human brain.

Point out the brain stem, cerebellum, and cerebrum and discuss the significance of each. Ask, "What could you do to remember this information? What part of your brain will you use to remember it?" Have students

---

*Any type of visual will help students to understand the complexity of the brain. Use posters, transparencies, books, videos, etc. instead of or in addition to models. Or invite students to create their own models or diagrams.

make up acronyms to help them remember the parts of the brain. (See pages 91–92 of the student book.)

5. Diagram a neuron. Label its parts and discuss its importance.

6. Conduct a simulation to review how the brain sends and receives messages.

Prepare 9 signs printed with the following words or phrases:

neuron	synapse
axon	dendrite
outgoing message	incoming message
electrical impulse	glial cells
chemical signal	

Give the signs to individual students. Explain that they will be demonstrating the process of how the brain sends and receives messages. They will "simulate" how a message begins in a neuron, how it travels, and where it goes. (*Summary:* A nerve impulse is transmitted along the nerve cell from dendrite to axon and then carried across the synapse by chemical neurotransmitters.) Allow time for the students to meet and decide how they will do their simulation. Have them present it to the class.

7. Begin creating a class Brain Trivia Game.

Prepare 2-3 sample questions on *green* 3" x 5" cards. For each, write the question on the front and the answer on the back.

SAMPLE QUESTIONS

What is the oldest part of the brain?

    a. cerebellum

    b. cerebrum

    c. brain stem

True or false?

    The bigger your brain is, the smarter you are.

Tell the students that they will create a Brain Trivia Game to play during the last session. (If the students are not familiar with trivia games, explain how they are played.) They will write the questions for the game, starting with the category, "Parts and Functions of the Brain." Show the sample questions you prepared.

Give each student several green 3" x 5" cards. Explain that they may base their questions on pages 1–22 of *It's All in Your Head*, and/or on other sources they find. Allow class time for students to write their questions. (Or assign this as a home project, and tell students to bring their question cards to the next class.) You may want to set a minimum on the number of questions students should write. They should give their completed question cards to you. Accumulate the cards in a file box for play during the final session.

Optional Activities

1. Research the history of the study of the human brain.

Compare what people knew about the brain 100 years ago with what we know today. Discuss methods and tools used by neuroscientists now and in the past.

2. Show a film or video about the evolution of the brain.

Recommended: *The Brain* (College/High School Level) series of eight videotapes. See Resources, page 41.

3. Using models or visuals, compare the human brain to an animal brain. Locate the major sections of the animal brain.

4. *Debate the question, "Do you think a computer could ever do everything the brain does?"*

Provide guidelines if students are not experienced debaters.   For example, they will need to research their positions so their arguments are based on established information, not personal opinion.

5. *Allow students to explore software on the brain.*

See Resources, page 42.

6. *Use a guided imagery exercise to help students visualize the inner workings of the brain.*

Relaxation exercise: "Close your eyes and think about your breathing....Take ten deep breaths.   Concentrate on each one....Continue your breathing, and focus your attention on your feet. Relax the muscles in your feet....Gradually work your way up your body. Relax the muscles in your legs...your torso...your arms and hands...your neck...your face....You should now be completely relaxed, from the tips of your toes to the top of your head."

SCRIPT: A JOURNEY THROUGH THE BRAIN

"You are now in a state of deep relaxation. You are a minute electrical impulse in your nervous system. As you begin to travel up your spinal cord, you proceed to the oldest part of your brain, the medulla or brain stem....

"As you stop to take a look around, you realize that this is the computer control center of your body....This is the area that is essential to keeping you alive. It controls your life-support systems such as sleep, body temperature, growth, perspiration, blood pressure and breathing....

"While you're trying to be careful in there, you also notice the pituitary gland, which is responsible for triggering hormones that control feelings like aggression and hunger....

"Let's try to monitor your heartbeat....Look at the computer monitor in your brain stem and watch what happens as you listen to your heartbeat....Listen carefully....Slow down your heartbeat....Watch your heartbeat as it slows down....Now speed it back up....

"Now that you're done playing around in the brain stem, keep traveling until you reach the brain itself....You are now moving into a gray and white gelatin-like substance that weighs about three and a half pounds....As you look around, you can see the curved bony skull which protects the brain....You're actually standing in the cerebellum, which resembles the shape of a butterfly....You're next to the brain stem and realize that this area controls the coordination and balance of your body....

"Look around....look at the millions of electrical wires that send messages to the muscles in your body and control your movements....Let's focus your electrical energy on the muscles in your left hand. Send a message to those muscles and tell them to slowly tighten your hand into a fist....then relax the hand.

"It's time to continue our journey, so carefully move your electric self through the endless maze of electrical connections that make up the cerebellum....Let's move into the youngest part of your brain, the cerebrum....

"The cerebrum sits on top of the brain stem and resembles a mushroom. The surface reminds you of a crumpled-up piece of paper, and the wrinkles allow more nerve cells to be stuffed into the skull....If your cerebrum were flattened out, it would actually cover one and one-half square feet!

"Standing on the very top of the cerebrum and looking down, you will notice that the cerebrum is divided into two equal parts, or hemispheres....The right side controls the left side of the body, and the left side controls the right....

"Look very carefully and you will find the corpus callosum, which resembles a bridge made of knotted ropes and connects the right and left hemispheres....Walk down to the bridge and move to the very middle of it. Look around you....What do you see?

"Carefully move through the deep crevices of the cerebrum and cross the corpus callosum slowly, taking one last look at the places you have been exploring....Trace your steps back through the cerebellum and into the computer center located in the medulla. Move toward the door leading to your spinal cord....but first, take one last look around. Bring some of those mental images back with you. Pass electrically through the spinal cord.

"Get back in touch with your breathing. You are returning to your place in the room. Imagine what it looked like before you closed your eyes. When you are ready, open your eyes."

Follow-up Activity: Have students illustrate what they visualized in an outline drawing of a brain. Some may choose to write a story or poem about a trip into their mind. Others may try using paint or other art materials to translate what they saw in their mind's eye. Have an optional sharing session.

INTELLIGENCE
AND THINKING

It's All in Your Head **pages 23–58**

INTELLIGENCE

It's All in Your Head **pages 23–43**

Concepts

1. Intelligence testing is a controversial issue for many reasons

2. Multiple intelligences should be considered when measuring or assessing levels of intelligence.

3. Our intelligence is the result of a combination of environmental and innate factors.

Materials

▶ Dictionaries

▶ Newsprint or other paper for brainstorming

▶ Brief quiz for experiment

▶ Yellow 3" x 5" index cards for Brain Trivia Game

▶ Sample Brain Trivia questions (see Activity #18, page 10)

▶ File box for Brain Trivia card storage

Activities

1. Define "intelligence."

Have students work individually or as a group to write their own definitions of "intelligence." Discuss their responses and compare with the definitions on pages 25–26 of the student book. Next, have students look up the word "intelligence" in one or more dictionaries. Compare dictionary definitions with student definitions.

2. Define "potential."

Have students write their own definitions of "potential," then look up the word in one or more dictionaries. Compare definitions. Ask, "How is potential related to intelligence?"

3. Name ways to measure human intelligence. Have students brainstorm a list of ideas.

4. Review the history of intelligence testing.

See pages 27–31 of the student book. Ask, "Why do you think people have spent so much time and effort inventing ways to measure intelligence?"

5. Define "I.Q."

Have students write their own definitions of "I.Q.," then look up "I.Q." and "intelligence quotient" in one or more dictionaries. Compare definitions.

6. Explore the topic of I.Q. scores and testing.

Possible discussion questions:

▶ In your opinion, is it helpful or harmful to know your own I.Q. score?

▶ Would you want to know your I.Q. score? Why or why not?

▶ Would you want someone else to know your I.Q. score? What people would you tell it to? What people wouldn't you tell it to?

▶ What are some ways in which people could use information about another person's I.Q. score?

▶ What are some positive effects of I.Q. testing?

▶ What are some negative effects of I.Q. testing?

▶ Why do people take I.Q. tests?

7. Explore the topic of standardized testing.

Discuss the differences between standardized *achievement* tests (examples: the Iowa Test of Basic Skills, the California Achievement Test) and standardized *aptitude* tests (examples: the Cognitive Abilities Test, the Structure of the Intellect Test). Cite as examples whichever tests are commonly given in your school. Ask, "Which type of test would you rather take? Why?" Review why your school gives standardized tests and how the results are used. Discuss the pros and cons of standardized testing. Record students' responses on a T-bar list.

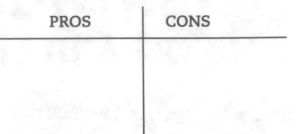

STANDARDIZED TESTS	
PROS	CONS

8. Conduct an experiment to show how outside influences may affect test results.

Distribute a brief test or quiz in any given subject area. Direct some of the students to take off their shoes; dim a few lights; have a few students trade pencils; read the directions very quickly; and/or invent your own "outside influences." Have students take the test or quiz. Discuss how your "outside influences" may have affected their performance.

9. Explore the idea that there are different ways of being "smart."

Have students brainstorm a list of talents or intelligences. Ask, "How can these be measured?"

10. Introduce the idea of nontraditional testing.

Some school districts, including one in Hinsdale, Illinois, and several in New York City, conduct "nontraditional" testing. For example, rather than give students paper-and-pencil science tests, these districts have devised hands-on science tests. Students demonstrate their knowledge and skills with magnets and thermometers, measuring cups and baking soda, etc. Rather than *tell* what they know in science, they *show* what they know by performing specific tasks.

Share this information with your students, then ask, "What do you think of hands-on tests as compared to paper-and-pencil tests? Which type seems most practical to you?"

11. *Design tests and evaluation methods.*

Divide the class into small groups of three or four. Give them the following instructions. Allow time for the teams to develop their ideas, then have each team present its ideas to the class. Discuss the pros and cons of each team's test and evaluation methods.

Instructions: "Your team has been hired by a major educational testing company to design a test which will measure multiple intelligences. The company would like you to come up with ways to test for a variety of talents in several areas such as music, art, athletics, leadership, creativity, science, and other academic areas. Come up with a plan to test the intelligences of school-age children nationwide. Then decide how you will evaluate the test results. How will you score the tests? What will the scores mean?"

12. *Discuss the issue of when (and whether) testing is actually necessary.*

Ask, "Are there any times when testing is a good idea? If you ran the school, what would you do about testing? Which tests would you eliminate? Which tests would you keep? Why?"

13. *Discuss the nature vs. nurture controversy.*

Ask, "What do you think has been most important in determining your own intelligence, genes or environment? Explain your answer." Review and discuss Dr. Marian Diamond's research on rats (student book page 39).

14. *Design a plan for an experiment.*

Divide the class into small groups of three or four. Give them the following instructions. Allow time for the teams to develop their plans, then have each team present its ideas to the class. Discuss the pros and cons of each team's plan.

Instructions: "Your team has been hired by a research company to design an experiment which will show how the environment affects brain development and/or intelligence. Start by formulating a hypothesis. Then write a description of how you would proceed with your experiment. Be as complete as you can."

15. *Link specific talents and skills to brain areas and functions.*

Tell the students to name a physical skill they are good at, such as a sport or a game, playing an instrument, dancing, etc. Ask them to identify the brain areas and functions that make each skill possible. It may help to break it down into parts: hand-eye coordination, movement, the senses, etc. Ask, "What could you do to develop this skill? What other physical skill or skills would you like to develop?"

16. *Review Gardner's list of multiple intelligences.*

See pages 41–43 of the student book. Ask, "Are there any intelligences Gardner may have forgotten? What else would you include?"

Ask, "Which type of intelligence do you feel is your personal strength? (It's okay to name more than one type.) Why do you feel this way? What can you do to enhance this intelligence?"

17. *Identify people who seem to "fit" one or more of Gardner's seven intelligences.*

Divide the class into small groups. Each group should have a "recorder"—someone who writes down everyone else's ideas as they say them. Tell the groups to brainstorm names of people (past or present, famous and not-so-famous) who seem to "fit" one or more of Gardner's intelligences, as shown in the examples below. It's okay if the same person's name appears on more than one list. Have the groups present their lists to the class.

Examples:

▶ *Linguistic:* Martin Luther King, Jr., Judy Blume

▶ *Musical:* Phil Collins, Kathleen Battle

▶ *Logical-Mathematical:* Einstein, Marie Curie

▶ *Spatial:* Leonardo da Vinci, Louise Nevelson

▶ *Bodily-Kinesthetic:* Michael Jordan, Steffi Graf

▶ *Interpersonal:* Mohandas Gandhi, Mother Theresa

▶ *Intrapersonal:* Carl Jung, Christa McAuliffe

18. Continue creating a class Brain Trivia Game.

Prepare 2-3 sample questions on *yellow* 3" x 5" cards to show to the class. Tell the students that this time they will be writing questions for the category, "Intelligence and Thinking." Show the sample questions. Give each student several yellow 3" x 5" cards. Keep accumulating the questions in a file box.

SAMPLE QUESTIONS

Of the following three people, which two have done work in the area of multiple intelligences?

    a. Robert Sternberg

    b. David Wechsler

    c. Howard Gardner

True or false?

    Scientists have proved that heredity is more important than environment in determining how smart someone is.

Optional Activities

1. Compare the intelligence of human beings with the intelligence of animals.

Have students research one or more of the following animals: chimpanzees, dolphins, dogs, birds. Or let them research animals of their choice.

2. Research the work of Dr. Marian Diamond.

3. Debate the nature vs. nurture controversy.

For example, students could form teams to debate the question of whether heredity is the major determinant of intelligence. One team could argue in support of this theory, while the other team could present research backing the other point of view.

LEFT-BRAIN AND RIGHT-BRAIN THINKING

It's All in Your Head pages 44–48

Concepts

1. Each half of the cerebrum is responsible for special functions, but the two halves cooperate for many of these functions.

2. The corpus callosum provides communication between the two hemispheres to transmit learning and memory.

Activities*

1. Have students "model" the brain with the hands.

Instructions: "Clench both hands into fists. Put your hands together at the first and second knuckles, with your thumbs toward your body. When your fists are in this position, they are the approximate size of your brain. Notice the two halves and look where the knuckles meet. In your brain, this connecting part is called the corpus callosum. Now look at the bumps created by the knuckles and veins. This looks a little like the neocortex, or outer brain layer."

2. Discuss left-brain and right-brain functions.

Ask, "Which half of your brain are you using right now, as you listen to me?" Have students name the functions of the left and right hemispheres. Record their responses on a list or a web, or have students create their own

*Many of the activities suggested in upcoming sections of this Teacher's Guide, particularly Problem-Solving and Thinking (pages 15–25) and Creativity (pages 31–34), also enhance right-brain thinking. You may want to look ahead to see if there are any you would like to include in this session.

graphic outlines of the two halves of the brain. Compare the functions and point out how the two hemispheres work together most of the time.

Review the examples on pages 46–47 of the student book. Have students think of more examples which demonstrate how the two hemispheres cooperate.

Ask the students to name famous people who exhibit strengths in left-hemisphere, right-hemisphere, and both-hemisphere activities.

3. Conduct an experiment to discover whether students' thinking tends to be left-brain dominant, right-brain dominant, or neither.

Dr. Jerre Levy, a researcher at the University of Chicago, has discovered a short, simple test for determining which side of a person's brain is dominant. Students will need writing paper and pencils.

Instructions: "Write a few words on a piece of paper—any words you choose. Use your normal writing hand and watch it as it moves. Is the pencil pointed toward you or away from you? Is your hand below the line of writing, or is it curled up above it?"

Explanation: People tend to use two main writing techniques: straight and hooked. Straight writers hold their hands below the line, with the pencil pointing away from them. Hooked writers curl their hand up over the line, with the pencil pointing toward them. Many left-handers are hooked writers. They may be conditioned to write this way so their hand won't smear their writing. Dr. Levy has found that how you write may reveal which side of your brain is dominant. *Straight right-handers* have a dominant left brain. *Straight left-handers* have a dominant right brain. *Hooked left-handers* have a dominant left brain. *Hooked right-handers* have a dominant right brain. (Dr. Levy's research seems to indicate that only straight writers have the normal criss-cross relationship between dominant brain and dominant hand.)

Follow-up Activity: Have students determine whether they are right-footed or left-footed. Ask, "Which foot do you jump on, kick with, or put forward first when walking, running, or doing sports? Are you right-footed or left-footed? Does this correlate with your handedness?"

4. Explore ways to bring right-brain thinking into traditionally left-brain activities.

Name (or have students name) subjects which involve left-brain thinking. For each, ask, "If you're a right-brain-dominant person, how can you make this subject easier for yourself?" Following are examples for a few subject areas. Share these with the students, and invite them to contribute their own examples for these and other subject areas.

▶ *Language arts.* Cut out letters for spelling words. Play Scrabble often.

▶ *Creative writing.* Think in images, pictures, and single words. Try to form associations before you begin writing.

▶ *Science.* As you learn the facts, try thinking intuitively as you do experiments. Make up fantasies or stories to help you remember scientific concepts.

▶ *Math.* Most math is considered to be a left-brain activity, but geometry is more of a right-brain function. Inventing geometric "shapes" to represent other math concepts may be one way to get the right brain involved.

5. Develop a plan for learning a new subject that involves both left-brain and right-brain functions.

Divide the class into small groups of three or four. Give them the following instructions. Allow time for the teams to develop their ideas, then have each team present its ideas to the class.

Instructions: "Think of something new you want to learn, or a subject you want to know more about. Develop a plan for accomplishing this task. Make sure that your plan covers these three areas, plus any others you think of and want to include: 1) Ways to learn that involve the left brain, the right brain, and both hemispheres at the same time. 2) Ways to learn that involve your memory, intuition, and senses. 3) Resources you might use to help you learn."

Optional Activities

1. Make posters illustrating the different ways the two hemispheres operate, and also how they cooperate.

2. Create life-size, three-dimensional clay models of the brain.

3. Design an experiment to demonstrate left-brain and right-brain functions.

Allow the students to work with partners or in small groups. Have them present their plans to the class. Discuss the pros and cons of each plan.

4. Find more self-tests related to left-brain and right-brain dominance.

There are several inventories available in various books. These usually involve answering a number of multiple-choice questions, then scoring yourself to discover your brain dominance preference. Students usually enjoy these quizzes, but they should understand from the outset that the results are not scientific or even very reliable. Their score may change from day to day.

5. Interview people to learn how they use left-brain and right-brain functions in their everyday lives.

Students who want to do this activity should plan to contact two or more people, then report their findings to the class.

Possible interview subjects:

artist	architect
accountant	sculptor
musician	athlete
parent	doctor
chef	dentist
photographer	teacher
bus driver	lawyer
dancer	detective
landscape designer	

Possible interview questions:

▶ How do you remember what you learn?

▶ How do you use your intuition in your daily work?

▶ Which of your senses do you use the most in your work?

▶ What problem-solving methods work best for you?

▶ Which seems to help you the most in your everyday life: your memory, intuition, senses, or problem-solving abilities?

MALE AND FEMALE BRAIN DIFFERENCES

It's All in Your Head pages 50–54

Concept

Sex differences in the human brain may be due to brain organization and environmental experiences.

Activities

1. *Review the controversial research on the topic of male/female brain differences.*

See pages 50–52 of the student book. Possible discussion questions:

▶ Do you agree or disagree with the idea that there are distinct differences between male and female brains?

▶ Which differences do you think are physiological, and which do you think are due to environmental influences?

▶ What can be done to change stereotypical thinking in the area of male and female brain differences?

▶ What can be done to encourage more females to enter math, science, and other technical fields? What's being done right now?

▶ What can be done to encourage more males to enter teaching, nursing, and other fields usually associated with females?

2. *Share personal experiences related to the way society perceives the female brain and the male brain—and, by extension, the abilities, strengths, potential, etc. of females and males.*

Invite open discussion of these issues. Ask students if they base their own expectations of a person's abilities on his or her gender.

Optional Activities

1. *Research the differences in how boys and girls are raised in our culture.*

Students should consult at least three different sources (books, magazines, etc.). They should decide whether they agree or disagree with the findings. Have them present their findings and opinions to the class.

2. *Research the ways the female brain and male brain have been perceived in the past.*

GENIUS

It's All in Your Head pages 55–58

Concept

Geniuses are often defined by their accomplishments.

Activities

1. *Name geniuses of the 20th century.*

Have students brainstorm a list of people from the 20th century they consider to be geniuses. For each, ask, "Why does this person belong on the list?"

2. *Predict geniuses of the 21st century.*

Have students project who will be the geniuses of the 21st century. List them by name and/or by future accomplishment. (*Example:* The person who finds a cure for cancer....The first colonist on Mars.) Discuss each one.

3. *Discuss Benjamin Bloom's study.*

See pages 57–58 of the student book. Ask, "Can you relate this to your own life? Has there ever been a time when your drive and determination helped you to succeed?" Discuss the relationship between potential and genius.

Optional Activity

Research and report on a genius.

Let students choose their subject. Have them research the person's early life, influences, and accomplishments. Have them report on their genius by writing an article for the school newspaper or presenting their information in some other way (example: acting the part of the genius in a one-person play). If several students choose this activity, consider publishing a class magazine or putting on a class play.

PROBLEM-SOLVING AND THINKING

It's All in Your Head **pages 59–81**

PROBLEM-SOLVING

It's All in Your Head **pages 59–61**

Concepts

1. Problem-solving skills can be learned and practiced.
2. Mastering problem-solving skills can help us to boost our brain power.

Materials

▶ Newsprint or other paper for brainstorming

▶ Poster or handout of the Creative Problem-Solving Process (see page 16)

Activities

1. Open with a general discussion of problems and problem-solving.

Ask, "What is a problem?" Personalize the discussion with questions like, "How do you solve problems?" and "What's the most difficult problem you have ever been faced with?

How did you solve it?" Since most problems are created inside our heads, ask students to think about a real or hypothetical problem. Invite them to brainstorm a list of problems.

2. Generate problem-solving tips.

Tell students to read the list on pages 60–61 of the student book. Divide the class into pairs or small groups and challenge them to come up with more tips to add to the list. Have them present their tips to the class.

3. Introduce and define the creative problem-solving process (CPS).

Prepare a poster or handout showing the creative problem-solving process developed by Sidney Parnes and Alex Osborn. A reproducible handout is found on page 16.

Ask, "Do you think it helps to have a process for solving problems—a special way to approach problems and deal with them? How does this compare to the way you usually solve problems?" Show the poster or distribute the handout. Then, since it's helpful to introduce this process by applying it to a real problem, share the following example of how CPS was used in one school.*

---

*See page 42 for additional resources on problem-solving. You'll find more explanations of the CPS process and ideas for activities to try with your students.

STEPS TO CREATIVE PROBLEM-SOLVING

I.   THE MESS   Identify the problem.

II. FACT-FINDING   Clarify the problem by listing the facts: who, what, when, where, why, how?

III. PROBLEM-FINDING   State the problem in many ways using IWWM statements: "**I**n **W**hat **W**ays **M**ight....?"

IV. IDEA-FINDING   Select the most important problem and restate it using IWWM. Brainstorm a list of solutions.

V.   SOLUTION-FINDING   Use a decision-making grid and criteria to find the best solution.

VI. ACCEPTANCE-FINDING   Write up a plan of action to implement your solution.

EXAMPLE

Step I: THE MESS

Too many paper products and plastic materials are being disposed of in the school cafeteria.

Step II: FACT-FINDING

▶ *Who* is involved in the situation? (Students, cafeteria workers, lunchroom supervisor, principal.)

▶ *What* does it involve? (Plastic utensils, straws, containers, paper plates, cups, bags, etc.)

▶ *When* is it happening? (Lunch hour, snack breaks.)

▶ *Where* is it happening? (School cafeteria.)

▶ *Why* is it happening? (People are bringing lunches which contain non-recyclable items; the cafeteria is selling too many paper and plastic products.)

Step III: PROBLEM-FINDING

▶ In **W**hat **W**ays **M**ight we reduce the amount of non-recyclable items being disposed of in the cafeteria? (IWWM statement.)

▶ IWWM we encourage people to bring or purchase lunches and snacks that come in recyclable packaging?

▶ IWWM we make people more aware of the seriousness of disposing of non-recyclable materials?

▶ IWWM we influence the cafeteria workers to decrease their sales of non-recyclable materials?

Step IV: IDEA-FINDING

IWWM we reduce the amount of non-recyclable items being disposed of in the cafeteria?

▶ Separate waste containers to separate trash; monitor how much is being disposed of

▶ Hold a student campaign to increase everyone's awareness of the situation

▶ Set rules and regulations for what items can be brought from home

▶ Have the cafeteria discontinue its use of non-recyclable materials

▶ Send a memo to parents, staff, and students about the current problem

▶ Have a contest or weekly goal to reduce the pounds of non-recyclable stuff being thrown away

▶ Show a tape or film which encourages the use of recyclables

Step V: SOLUTION-FINDING

CRITERIA
Which idea will be the...

IDEAS	Longest lasting?	Least costly?	Most effective?	Easiest to implement?	TOTAL
Separate trash	3	5	2	5	15
Student campaign	1	2	4	2	9
Cafeteria discontinues use	5	4	1	3	13
Contest	2	1	3	1	7
Educate students, staff & parents	4	3	5	4	(16)

Rating Scale: 1-5

5 = most favorable idea

1 = least favorable idea

The idea with the highest total is the most favorable.

Step VI: ACCEPTANCE-FINDING

Using the given criteria, "educate students, staff & parents" appears to be the most favorable solution to the original problem: "In what ways might we reduce the amount of non-recyclable items being disposed of in the cafeteria?"

In order to make students, staff, and parents more aware of the current situation, we would design a step-by-step awareness campaign to discourage the use of non-recyclable items.

▶ First, we would create and post large signs throughout the school.

▶ Second, we would publish an informational flyer for the entire student body, staff, and parents.

▶ Third, we would have students and staff view a videotape which highlights the advantages of using recyclables and shows the serious long-term effects of disposal of non-recyclable materials.

▶ Finally, at the end of the awareness campaign, we would hold a "RECYCLABLES ONLY" lunch day, where each person would be encouraged to bring only recyclable items in their lunches. Also, the cafeteria would use only recyclable packaging and other items that day.

As a follow-up to this activity, we would continue to encourage this practice on a daily basis by having contests or weekly goals to reduce the amount of non-recyclable trash.

4. *Explore more ways of using CPS.*

Tell students that this problem-solving process can be applied to many different situations. Once they learn the steps, they can use it at home, in the classroom—wherever there are problems to solve! Ask, "Who has ideas for where and how you might try creative problem-solving?"

Optional Activity

Encourage students to participate in inventing contests, the Future Problem-Solving Program, and/or Odyssey of the Mind.

▶ Future Problem Solving Program, Arbor Atrium, 315 West Huron, Suite 140-B, Ann Arbor, MI 48103.

▶ Odyssey of the Mind Program, OM Association, PO Box 27, Glassboro, NJ 08028.

▶ INVENT AMERICA! Contest, 510 King Street, Suite 420, Alexandria, VA 22314.

▶ Weekly Reader National Inventing Contest, 25 Long Hill Road, Middletown, CT 06457. Attention: Dr. Irwin Siegelman, Editorial Director. Telephone: (203) 638-2400.

THINKING

It's All in Your Head **pages 62–81**

Concepts

1. Learning about how and why we think the way we do can lead to personal discoveries about our potential abilities.

2. The human brain is capable of many types of thinking.

Materials

▶ Newsprint or other paper for "Tower of Pulp" activity

▶ Transparent tape

▶ Scissors

▶ "13 Ways to Sharpen Your Listening Skills" handout

Activities

1. Introduce the topic with the "Tower of Pulp" activity.

Give each student two sheets of newsprint or similar paper and two feet of transparent tape. Say, "Your task is to construct the *tallest* tower you can in fifteen minutes. You may cut, fold, or shape your materials any way you like." *Variation:* Have students construct the *longest* bridge.

Follow-up Activity: Discuss the thought processes they used to construct their tower or bridge. Ask, "Did you 'see' your tower/bridge in your mind before you started building it? What did you do first—see, think, or act?" Compare their thought processes. Which seemed to produce the best (tallest, longest) results? Continue the discussion with questions like these:

▶ Why is it important to learn how we think?

▶ What kind of thinking do you like to do?

▶ What did you learn about your own way of thinking from this activity?

2. Use one or more of the following activities to explore imagination and visualization.*

▶ "Imagination, the total of all you know and have experienced, is at the center of your being." Robert H. McKim. Read this quotation aloud and ask, "What do you think this means?"

▶ Read aloud the following list of people and things, one at a time and pausing after each one. Tell the students to try to see each one in their mind's eye as you name it. Ask them to rate their own visual imagery ability. Say, "Give yourself a 'C' if the image is clear in your mind—very sharp and detailed. Give yourself a 'V' if it's vague—fuzzy and without much detail. Give yourself an 'N' if you don't see anything." Tell the students not to worry if they don't see many (or any) sharp, detailed images; developing a sensory imagination takes time and practice.

    Your best friend's face

    Your bedroom

    A tulip

    The mailbox at your home

    A galloping horse

    A ferris wheel at a carnival

    Your first bike

    A space shuttle

    An early morning sunrise on the beach.

▶ Ask students to close their eyes, visualize their home, and count the number of windows they "see." Discuss what they discovered from this activity.

---

*See page 42 for additional resources on imagination and visual thinking.

▶ Ask students to close their eyes and envision a desired goal. (You may want to prepare them for this activity with the relaxation exercise on page 5.) Guide them toward visualizing themselves achieving this goal in the here-and-now. Afterward, ask, "What positive feelings did you experience while you were picturing your goal?"

SCRIPT: PICTURING YOUR GOAL

"Picture your goal in your mind....Now picture it as something you have already achieved.... For example, if you want to be an ace tennis player or a lead character in play, envision being that right now....Try to make your mental pictures vivid and detailed....Pay attention to the senses involved: the sights, sounds, feelings, tastes, smells of having reached your goal....The more vivid or intense you can make it, the better....Soon it may start to feel like the real thing."

3. Use one or more of the following activities to explore logical thinking.*

Logic activities use arguments, reasoning, and deductions. Have students look at a logical sequence of elements to discover if an idea or a situation makes sense. They will quickly recognize that logical thinking involves drawing conclusions based on certain known facts.

Before starting the activities, share these simple tips for solving logic problems:

▶ Draw a picture.

▶ Get enough information.

▶ Follow the premises.

▶ Start using logic in your everyday life.

▶ **Analogies.** Give students practice in creating analogies. Start with an example or two, then challenge them to make up their own.

Kennel is to dog as garage is to _____.

Swimming is to pool as _____ is to _____.

_____ is to _____ as _____ is to _____.

▶ **Inferences.** Inferences involve codes, hidden messages, word transformations, symbols, and ideas that follow predetermined rules.

Review several codes and place a message on the board or overhead transparency. Examples:

▶ Insert a letter in each space to form a familiar sequence.

d__rem__fas__llat__d__

HINT: All letters are vowels.

(*Answer:* The sequence is the musical scale: do, re, mi, fa, sol, la, ti, do.)

▶ The same letter is missing 15 times in the jumble of letters below. What is the letter? Insert it in the appropriate places and separate the words formed to uncover a factual statement.

nrdvrksmmmlththsshrpclwsndttcksnts

(*Answer:* The missing letter is "a." The statement is: An aardvark is a mammal that has sharp claws and attacks ants.)

▶ What is the next symbol in the following sequence?

(*Answer:* The sequence is the letters A-F. The right-hand portion of each symbol is the letter. The left-hand portion is the mirror image of the letter. So the next symbol in the sequence is F and its mirror image.)

---

*See page 42 for additional resources on logical thinking.

▶ **Deduction.** Invite students to experiment with these patterns. Remind them to make sure that their facts are correct, or their deductive "reasoning" won't make any sense! Tell them to be careful not to make false assumptions when using this argument. Say, "Sometimes you have to think about how illogical something is before you can understand logical thinking."

(1) All _____ are _____.

(2) All _____ are _____.

(3) Therefore, all _____ are _____.

(1) All _____ are _____.

(2) _____ is a _____.

(3) Therefore, all _____ are _____.

(*Example:* All B's are C. A is a C. Therefore, A is a B.)

4. *Explore and discuss intuition.*

Since intuition is innate, it doesn't require logic and reasoning. Instead, it's the quick recognition *from within* of how and why things are the way they are. Intuition can include three main components: common sense, sensitivity, and luck. It really isn't something you can "teach," but you can help your students to become more conscious of their intuition by encouraging them to "tune in" to it as they go about their daily lives. Suggest that they try one or more of the following activities:

▶ Tune into time. Stop wearing a watch or looking at a clock for a week.

▶ Tune into the weather. Jot down your feelings.

▶ Read mystery novels. After each chapter, write down who you suspect and why.

▶ Tune into yourself. Write down your guesses and hunches about anything and everything, from "Who will win the World Series?" to "Will the math test be easy or hard?"

▶ Take guesses before you measure with an instrument. Compare your guesses to the actual measurements.

Ask, "What do you think will happen if you (stop wearing a watch, start reading mysteries, etc.)? Can you think of other activities to add to this list?"

5. *Try "productive daydreaming."*

Explain that there are two kinds of daydreamers: those who daydream to escape from reality, and those who practice "productive daydreaming." These visual thinkers daydream for purposeful reasons. In other words, not all daydreaming is "bad." Sometimes it can be quite useful. And since most people daydream anyway, we may as well teach our students how to use this thinking technique to their advantage.

Dim the lights, quiet the room, and lead the students in a relaxation exercise such as the one on page 5. Guide them into thinking about a subject they would like to think about more productively. Tell them just to follow their thoughts wherever they lead. They should not try to direct their thoughts or reach any particular conclusion. Afterward, discuss their experience. *Note:* This activity may be more effective right before bedtime or when they first wake up in the morning. It may not work in a classroom setting.

6. *Explore and experience pattern thinking.*

Brain patterns are made up of interrelated information which produces an expected outcome. We experience them as predispositions, preconceptions, or mind sets. Pattern thinking is stronger than we realize. Most patterns are programmed into us, so they are usually easy to remember.

How much do we depend on pattern thinking? Find out by trying the following activities. Share them with your students. See who can come up with the right answer first. (The answers are on page 25.)

▶ Look at this sequence of numbers. What is the basis for their progression?

8 1 6 4 3 7 0 1 2

► All of the letters of the alphabet are arranged along this line—except for the Z. Where does the Z go, above the line or below it?

A		EF	HI	KLMN		T	VWXY
	BCD	G		J	OPQRS	U	

Have students tell about the patterns in their own lives. Is there something they always "see" in the same way, even though there are many possible ways to "see" it?

7. Use one or more of the following activities to explore the relationship between listening and thinking.

► Ask, "On a scale of 1-10, with 1 being the lowest and 10 being the highest, how would the following people rate you as a listener? Remember: this is what *they* think of *you*."

Your best friend.

Your mother.

Your home room teacher.

Your father.

Your brothers or sisters.

► Discuss the saying, "It goes in one ear and out the other." Ask, "Do you know anyone who fits this description? Why is it important to learn how to listen?"

► Prepare a handout, "13 Ways to Sharpen Your Listening Skills." Give copies to the students and ask them to practice these techniques at home. A reproducible handout is found on page 24.

Optional Activities

1. For imagination and visualization.

Following a relaxation exercise (see page 5), play different types of music (jazz, classical, rock, New Age, etc.). Have students listen for a short period, then draw pictures which represent the images they "saw" for each style of music. Afterward, discuss and compare the similarities and differences in their pictures. Ask, "Why did the different types of music evoke different images?"

Have students select one or two imagination and visual thinking exercises they would like to lead for the class. This will involve some research and planning on their part; you may want to point them toward the Resources (page 42). They might try relating their exercise(s) to a current unit of study in the classroom.

2. For logical thinking.

Students may want to create their own logic problems after trying the examples. The following resources may provide inspiration as well as challenging fun.

► *Adventures With Logic (Grades 5-7)* by Mark Schoenfield and Jeannette Rosenblatt. Available from Fearon Teaching Aids, 500 Harbor Blvd., Belmont, CA 94002.

► *Logic (Kindergarten-Grade 9)* by Hands-On, Inc., 2121 Rebild Drive, Solvang, CA 93463.

► A series of books by Anita Harnadek contain a variety of inference, deduction, and general problem-solving activities. They are available from Midwest Publications, PO Box 129, Troy, MI 48099.

3. For intuition.

Have those students who try the activities listed under #4, page 22 report on their experiences of "tuning in" to their intuition.

13 WAYS TO SHARPEN YOUR LISTENING SKILLS

1. Tune your mind and ears to all sounds in the environment.

2. Exercise! It improves all of your senses.

3. Listen longer.

4. Search for more "advanced" (challenging) materials.

5. Actively work at remembering.

6. Use *synesthesia:* Blend your senses. When you are listening, keep your other senses—especially sight—actively involved.

7. Keep an open mind.

8. Use brainspeed. Use your brain power to organize, summarize, and hear between the lines.

9. Listen to the content. Disregard the way it's said.

10. Listen for themes rather than individual facts.

11. Take notes using a "webbing" technique. (This is a form of brainstorming that uses a graphic "web.")

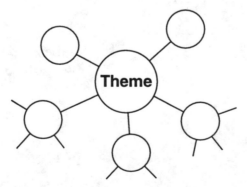

12. Ignore distractions.

13. Try to visualize and imagine what you are hearing.

4. For daydreaming.

Have those students who try productive day-dreaming at home report on their experiences.

5. For pattern thinking.

Have students search for more "patterns" in their everyday life. They will probably recognize that patterns can be found everywhere—math, science, history, language arts, music, art, technology, etc.

6. For listening.

Using "13 Ways to Sharpen Your Listening Skills" (see page 24), have a "listening morning" or a "listening afternoon." Tell students to try some of these suggestions during a typical school day. Ask them to report on their discoveries and experiences.

Answers to Problems on Pages 22–23

▶ Sequence of numbers. Most people try to solve this mathematically, but the sequence is actually based on the shapes of the numbers. Did you notice that every other number has a curve in it?

▶ The Z goes above the line. Just as in the sequence of numbers problem, the answer is based on the shapes of the letters. All those below the line are curved.

MEMORY AND LEARNING

It's All in Your Head pages 82–95

Concepts

1. Several types of memory exist and are stored throughout the brain wherever they are processed.

2. There may be different memory structures for acquiring skills and for remembering specific events and facts.

Materials

▶ High-quality color reproduction of a painting (preferably one with lots of detail)

▶ Blue 3" x 5" index cards for Brain Trivia Game

▶ Sample Brain Trivia questions (see Activity #7, page 29)

▶ File box for Brain Trivia card storage

Activities

1. Introduce the topic with a memory exercise.

Show students the reproduction of the painting for 45 seconds. Say, "Try to remember as much of this painting as you can. Try seeing it as a pattern. Look carefully at the details. Follow outlines and note the features. Now close your eyes and visually recall what you saw....Open your eyes and compare what you remember with the actual painting." Repeat 2-3 more times and evaluate whether the images students remember are improving in terms of clarity and accuracy. Try the activity with other objects or scenes in the classroom. Discuss how memory and seeing are mutually reinforcing.

2. Discuss the six types of memory.

Review the descriptions on pages 85–87 of the student book. Ask, "What type of memory did you use in the first activity?" (Short-term memory.)

3. Introduce ways to improve the memory.

Tell students that within a 24-hour period, we forget almost 80 percent of what we read or hear. Ask, "If this is true, how can we improve our ability to remember? How can we transfer information from short-term memory to long-term memory? What do you think you need before you can remember something?"

Present these three basic guidelines for improving the memory:

▶ *Visualize.* Picture what you want to remember. Become observant!

▶ *Repeat.* Say it over and over again.

▶ *Associate.* Use cues and clues to connect new information you want to remember to old information you already remember.

Ask students to share their own ideas or tricks for remembering information. Which techniques seem to work the best?

4. Introduce an example of a mnemonic technique such as the Number-Rhyme System.

In this system, you devise key memory images represented by a word that rhymes with the sound of the number. For example, "5" rhymes with "hive."

NUMBER	NUMBER-SOUND MEMORY WORD
1	sun, bun, gun
2	shoe, crew, gnu
3	tree, knee, flea
4	door, moor, boar
5	hive, dive, chive
6	sticks, bricks
7	heaven
8	date, gate
9	fine, line, wine
10	den, hen, pen

Ask students how they can apply this technique to a particular subject or topic in order to improve their recall of ideas.

Have students share any other mnemonic techniques they may already be using. (These will probably be variations of the following systems, and some may overlap or seem similar.)

▶ Link system

▶ Picture-rhyme association

▶ Acronyms and acrostics (acronyms are described on pages 91–92 of the student book)

▶ The LOCI technique (described on pages 92–94 of the student book)

▶ Chunking

▶ Number-alphabet system

▶ Mind mapping.

Students might be interested in searching for further information regarding mnemonic techniques. See page 43 for suggested books.

5. Use mnemonics to teach a topic or concept.

Divide the class into pairs. Give them the following instructions. Allow time for students to choose their topic and mnemonic technique, then have them teach their topic to the class in mini-lessons. Evaluate the techniques. Ask, "Which ones seemed to work best? Which ones would you use again?" Discuss the possible drawbacks of mnemonic devices.

Instructions: "Choose a subject you would like to teach. Then choose a particular topic or concept from that subject. Next, choose one thing about your topic or concept you want everyone to learn. For example, if your subject is Science, you might narrow that down to light and optical illusions. Then you might decide that everyone should learn the parts of the eye. Select a mnemonic technique for teaching about the parts of the eye. Decide how you will present it to the class."

6. Introduce other important features of memory, and provide more memory tips.

Describe and discuss the following:

▶ Concentration and focused attention. (Does it matter if you're paying attention?)

▶ Desire and interest. (Does it matter if this is something you really want to learn?)

▶ Organization of thoughts. (Does it matter if you're thinking about a million different things at once?)

Present these memory tips:

▶ Learn material by understanding it. Don't just cram facts into your head.

▶ When studying, take short breaks every hour or so.

▶ Study before a nap.

▶ Relax! Reduce stress by exercising and practicing breathing techniques.

▶ Memorize out loud. Read the passage several times and paraphrase it in your own words.

▶ Work when you are most alert.

▶ Use all of your senses to memorize.

▶ Make it fun!

7. Continue creating a class Brain Trivia Game.

Prepare 2-3 sample questions on *blue* 3" x 5" cards to show to the class. Tell the students that this time they will be writing questions for the category, "Memory and Learning." Show the sample questions. Give each student several blue 3" x 5" cards. Keep accumulating the questions in a file box.

SAMPLE QUESTIONS

Which of these is NOT stored in short-term memory?

a. meanings of words you use daily

b. science facts you "crammed" for Friday's test

c. weekly spelling words

True or false?

Scientists have found that memory is located in a very specific part of the brain.

Optional Activity

Have students select one of the following topics (or another of their choosing) and research the latest findings. Have them share their findings with the group.

▶ Memory foods

▶ Memory pills and drugs

▶ Alzheimer's disease and senility

▶ Effects of alcohol and nicotine on memory

▶ Amnesia.

CREATIVITY

It's All in Your Head pages 96–114

Concepts

1. Creativity can be revitalized, developed, and strengthened through practice.
2. Learning to be more creative has enormous benefits for all ages.

Materials

▶ Dictionaries

▶ Newsprint or other paper for brainstorming and drawing

▶ Pink 3" x 5" index cards for Brain Trivia Game

▶ Sample Brain Trivia questions (see Activity #11, page 33)

▶ File box for Brain Trivia card storage

Activities

1. Define "creativity."

Have students work individually or as a group to write their own definitions of "creativity," then look up the word in one or more dictionaries. Compare definitions. Ask questions like the following to stimulate discussion:

▶ Can creativity be measured? Why or why not?

▶ What is the most creative thing you've done in your lifetime?

▶ Have you ever taken a creativity test? Do you think the results are a true indication of how creative you are?

▶ What does it mean to "dare to be different?"

2. Discuss creative people.

Have students name people they consider to be creative. Have them brainstorm a list of characteristics that creative people seem to have. Discuss the pros and cons of each characteristic.

3. Discuss what tends to happen to creativity as people get older.

Draw a dot on the board, then ask, "What is this?" The number of ideas students come up with often depends on their age. When this activity was done with a group of high-school sophomores, most students simply responded, "A dot on the board." When it was done with a group of kindergarten students, responses included "a pebble," "a cigar butt," "a rotten egg," "a squashed bug," etc.

Ask, "What happens to our creativity as we get older? Why does it seem to dry up when people become adults?" Tell students that they can continue being creative—and become more creative—if that's what they choose to do.

4. Consider ways in which creative people come up with their ideas.

Review the examples on page 99 of the student book. Ask, "Why do you think these strange behaviors helped?" Ask students to share any unusual "habits" or routines that help them to be more creative. Can they explain why these behaviors seem to work for them?

5. Discuss the "invisible fences" that block creativity.

Review the examples on pages 103–106 of the student text. Ask, "Can you think of other 'invisible fences' that get in the way of creative thinking? What is your biggest fear when it comes to being creative?" Discuss the power of positive thinking to overcome these "invisible fences."

Tell students to look at the 9-dot problem on page 104 of the student book (or write the problem on the board). Relate this problem to the idea that we sometimes get stuck in a rut when we are trying to find solutions. Sometimes we need to look beyond invisible boundaries and see things from a different point of view.

If students enjoy the 9-dot problem, give them a similar problem. Draw the following pattern on the board. Tell students to recreate using one continuous line. They can't lift their pencil off the paper, and they can't retrace any of the lines.

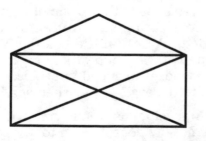

6. Define "convergent thinking" and "divergent thinking."

See pages 105–106 of the student book. Review the examples. Model at least one convergent question and one divergent question from a particular subject area. For example, questions for social studies might be:

▶ *Convergent:* What is the capital of the United States?

▶ *Divergent:* What if the capital of the United States were moved to Boise, Idaho?

Have students work in pairs or small groups to create their own convergent and divergent questions, then present them to the class. Ask questions like the following to stimulate discussion:

▶ Which kind of question do you prefer to answer? Why?

▶ Which answers are easier to evaluate? Which are more obviously "right" or "wrong"?

▶ If you could design a test, would you include more convergent or divergent questions? Why?

7. Explore ways to become more creative.

Review J.P. Guilford's four creative "products"—fluency, flexibility, originality, and elaboration—on pages 106–107 of the student book. Reinforce learning by sharing the following example.

EXAMPLE
Topic: Birds

▶ FLUENCY: Brainstorm a list of ideas related to the topic.

Example: Think of as many feathered creatures as you can.

▶ FLEXIBILITY: Come up with a variety of categories related to the topic.

Example: Group the creatures according to characteristics—what color feathers? Long or short beaks? Land creatures or water creatures?

▶ ORIGINALITY: Come up with clever, unique, and uncommon ideas related to the topic.

Example: Invent and illustrate a new kind of feathered creature.

▶ ELABORATION: Build on your ideas by expanding them, adding details, and refining them.

Example: Combine two kinds of creatures to create a new type of feathered animal. Add many details.

Ask, "How can you apply these skills to the more advanced topics you are studying? How can you apply them to a hobby, interest, challenge, or problem in your life?"

Review and discuss "Twenty Ways to Become More Creative than You Already Are" on pages 107–109 of the student book. Ask students to add their own ideas to this list.

8. *Review and discuss the inventing process.*

See page 111 of the student book. Ask students to think of one or more things they would like to invent. Ask, "How would your invention help to meet a need or solve a problem?"

9. *Review and discuss the SCAMPER technique.*

See pages 112–113 of the student book. Explain that SCAMPER can help us to see things in new and different ways. Have students suggest more objects to SCAMPER.

10. *Introduce Synectics as a way to stimulate creative thinking.*

Synectics is a technique for looking at familiar things in novel ways. W.J. Gordon came up with this idea for "making the familiar strange" and "making the strange familiar." The word *synectics* comes from the Greek and means "to join together different and irrelevant ideas." Many large corporations use this technique as a way to devise ideas for new products.

Synectics uses metaphor and analogy to stimulate creative thinking. It asks questions that compel us to look at ordinary objects and ideas in new and different ways. For example:

▶ How is a fuel filter like a human kidney?

▶ How is the brain like a machine?

▶ What animal is like a rubber band?

▶ What kind of animal are you most like?

▶ What do you know that's like a tree?

▶ Which is louder, a wink or a smile?

▶ Which is faster, the wind or gossip?

▶ Which is more tender, a word or a feeling?

▶ Which is more athletic, a fjord or a straight?

Questions like these are used as warm-ups, typically in a small group problem-solving setting. Some teachers use synectics-like questions to close a lesson. For example, "In what ways are autobiographies like ponds?" (One possible response: They both reflect.)

Try some of the sample questions with your students. Have them brainstorm questions to share with the group.

11. *Continue creating a class Brain Trivia Game.*

Prepare 2-3 sample questions on *pink* 3" x 5" cards to show to the class. Tell the students that this time they will be writing questions for the category, "Creativity and Creative People." Show the sample questions. Give each student several pink 3" x 5" cards. Keep accumulating the questions in a file box.

SAMPLE QUESTIONS

Which of the following was a famous scientist?

    a. Rudyard Kipling

    b. Marian Anderson

    c. Galileo

True or false?

Creative people have bigger, more advanced brains than other people.

Optional Activities

1. Research and report on a creative person.

Let students choose someone who especially interests them. They may want to learn more about a poet, an artist, a musician, a scientist, an inventor, a favorite author, etc. An excellent resource to get them started is *Creative Encounters with Creative People* by Janice Gudeman. Write to: Good Apple, Inc., 1204 Buchanan St., Box 299, Carthage, IL 62321. Telephone: (217) 357-3981.

You may want to direct students to research the kinds of problems their subjects had, how they overcame them, and how the creative process worked for them. Ask, "How are these people 'different' from most other people?" Have students design a creative way to share what they learned with the group.

2. Teach an interdisciplinary inventing unit.

This gives students the opportunity to discover and invent unique ideas which are meaningful to them. Interested students may want to get involved in one or more national inventing contests. Those listed below have been expanding each year and may be worth looking into. Most are open to students in grades K-12.

▶ Weekly Reader National Inventing Contest, 25 Long Hill Road, Middletown, CT 06457. Attention: Dr. Irwin Siegelman, Editorial Director. Telephone: (203) 638-2400.

▶ INVENT AMERICA! Contest, 510 King Street, Suite 420, Alexandria, VA 22314.

3. Use guided imagery and visualization to stimulate and enhance creativity.

See page 42 for resources that will help you use these techniques in your classroom. *Note:* If you already use guided imagery and visual-ization in your classroom, then you know how these techniques can enhance right-brain thinking and imagination skills. If you have never used them before but are considering trying them, resist the temptation to do a few "fun" activities now and then. It can be more worthwhile to integrate these techniques into your regular curriculum so students can see the connections and applicability to their everyday life.

4. Try metaphorical teaching.

With the current emphasis on thematic and interdisciplinary teaching, metaphorical teaching can be a powerful tool. Like synectics, it emphasizes connections: how a new idea or subject is like one that may already be understood. It focuses on the process of understanding patterns and principles which give more meaning to specific facts. Teaching through metaphor is a more "holistic" way to facilitate learning.

Begin by looking for two subject areas that can be integrated. For example, let's suppose your class is studying the local history of your town. Specifically, you're learning about how your town has grown through the years. How about relating this study to science—specifically, the growth of amphibians? However you choose to approach metaphorical teaching, remember that the process of making connections is more important than the specific content of a lesson.

Answer to Problem on Page 32

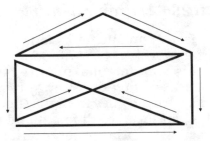

TLC FOR YOUR BRAIN

It's All In Your Head **pages 115–122**

Concepts

1. The health of the brain can vary according to the treatment it receives.

2. Rest, physical exercise, and a well-balanced diet are vital to maintaining a healthy brain and bolstering intelligence.

Materials

▶ Personal Health Self-Evaluation handout (see Activity #3, pages 35–36)

▶ White 3" x 5" index cards for Brain Trivia Game

▶ Sample Brain Trivia questions (see Activity #4, page 36)

▶ File box for Brain Trivia card storage

▶ Guidelines for the Brain Trivia Game (see page 37)

Activities

1. Find out how students "take care of their brains."

Ask, "What do you on a daily basis to make sure your brain stays healthy?" Discuss the importance of "TLC" (Tender Loving Care) for the brain. See if students can think of an analogy or metaphor to describe how they take care of their brain.

2. Discuss the relationship between mental, emotional, and physical health.

Ask, "How do stress, exercise, food, sleep, etc. affect a person's overall well-being? For example, what if you exercise regularly but don't sleep enough?" Encourage students to see that good health is the result of many factors, all interrelated. Stimulate discussion with questions like:

▶ When you are sick, how does it affect your mental performance?

▶ When you're feeling "down" emotionally, how does it affect your physical and mental condition?

3. Have students complete a Personal Health Self-Evaluation.

Prepare a handout including several health-related self-evaluation questions. You may want to do this in cooperation with the school nurse or health teacher. (Or you may find that a handout already exists for you to use with your students.) Questions might include:

▶ Do you wake up feeling refreshed in the morning?

▶ Can you run the length of two blocks without getting out of breath?

▶ Are you the right weight for your height and body type?

▶ Are your hair, skin, and nails in good condition?

Distribute the handout and have students complete it in class. Afterward, ask, "Which of these three areas do you need to work on the most: rest, exercise, or diet?"

4. Finish creating a class Brain Trivia Game.

Prepare 2-3 sample questions on *white* 3" x 5" cards to show to the class. Tell the students that this time they will be writing questions for the category, "Health and the Brain." Show the sample questions. Give each student several white 3" x 5" cards. If you plan to play the game today, allow students to work in pairs to write their questions. Collect the completed questions and add them to the others already accumulated in your file box.

SAMPLE QUESTIONS

One study showed that students who ate a good breakfast...

   a. got lower test scores

   b. got higher test scores

   c. breakfast didn't seem to make any difference

True or false?

   Some sugar can be good for you.

5. Play Brain Trivia.

Prepare a handout of the Guidelines to give to the class. A reproducible handout is found on page 37.

Optional Activities

1. Research recent findings on rest, exercise, and diet.

Have students come up with ways to improve their current habits. They may want to work in pairs or groups to present their findings to the class.

2. Design and implement a personal improvement plan.

Suggest that students design a plan that lasts long enough to make a difference—ideally, 6 to 9 weeks. They should try to fit their plan to their lifestyle, needs, and interests. At the end of their "experiment" period, have them report on their results. (Give them permission to keep personal goals private.)

An ambitious group may choose to write a script and perform a play about how to maintain a healthy brain through proper rest, exercise, and diet.

Example: To eat more nutritious foods.

   a. Research the nutritional value of foods I now eat.

   b. Decide what foods are missing from my diet.

   c. Research vitamins. Decide if I should be taking vitamin supplements.

   d. Keep a daily journal of what I eat.

   e. Stop eating junk food.

   f. At the end of 6 weeks, look back over my journal. How have my eating habits changed?

   g. Decide how my new plan has affected my overall emotional, mental, and physical well-being.

GUIDELINES FOR BRAIN TRIVIA

Materials needed:

File box with question cards in the following 5 categories:

1) Parts and Functions of the Brain (green cards)

2) Intelligence and Thinking (yellow cards)

3) Memory and Learning (blue cards)

4) Creativity and Creative People (pink cards)

5) Health and the Brain (white cards).

Object of the game:

To score the most points by correctly answering questions about the brain.

Scoring:

A correct answer is worth 1 point.

How to play:

Form teams of 2 or more players. Decide which team will go first ("Team A"). Team A selects a category, and another team (or the teacher) reads aloud a question from that category. If Team A answers correctly, they receive 1 point and get to choose another question from any category. Play continues until Team A misses a question and the turn passes to the next team ("Team B").

The rules:

1. Team members must reach consensus before giving an answer. In other words, they must *agree* on their answer. The team captain says the answer.

2. In Round 1, team members have 30 seconds to reach consensus. Round 1 is limited to 10 minutes.

3. In Round 2, team members have 15 seconds to reach consensus. Round 2 is limited to 5 minutes.

The winner:

Add up the points to determine the winning team.

Example: To avoid foods with additives.

    a. Research food additives and their effects.

    b. Learn how to read labels on packaged foods.

    c. Start reading labels on the foods I buy.

    d. Try not to eat foods with additives. Eat fresh, natural foods instead.

    e. Research nutritious, healthy snacks and learn how to prepare several.

    f. Keep a daily journal of what I eat.

    g. At the end of 6 weeks, look back over my journal. How have my eating habits changed?

    h. Decide how my new plan has affected my overall emotional, mental, and physical well-being.

3. Do extensive research on a related topic.

Invite students to thoroughly research a topic that interests them. Examples: the effects of toxic metals on the brain; how the abuse of alcohol and other drugs affects the brain; etc. Direct them toward a variety of printed resources, audiovisuals, and human resources—experts on their chosen topic. Have them present their projects in creative ways. Ideas for possible products include:

▶ slide-tape presentations

▶ videotapes

▶ display boards

▶ pamphlets

▶ posters

▶ transparencies

▶ skits or plays

▶ books

▶ rap songs

▶ musical performances.

ENDING
THE UNIT

Some students may be interested in learning more about other topics introduced in the student book:

▶ Biofeedback and Hypnosis (pages 123–127)

▶ Sleep and Dreams (pages 128–137)

▶ Mysteries of the Mind (pages 138–139).

Schedule a trip to the library to find books and articles. Or arrange for students to interview experts: psychologists, counselors, authors, psychiatrists, professors, physicians, and others who specialize in these and other brain-related topics. One or more of these professionals may be willing to visit your class for a presentation and a question-and-answer session.

If you haven't yet played the Brain Trivia Game, you may want to end the unit with it. Invite students to continue creating questions, and make this game a regular enrichment activity in your classroom.

RESOURCES

The Amazing Brain

Buzan, Tony. *Make the Most of Your Mind.* New York: Linden Press/Simon and Schuster, 1984.
— *Use Both Sides of Your Brain.* New York: E.P. Dutton, 1983.

Caine, Renate Nummela, and Geoffrey Caine. *Making Connections: Teaching and the Human Brain.* Alexandria, VA: Association for Supervision and Curriculum Development, 1991.

Ehrenberg, Marian, and Otto Ehrenberg. *Optimum Brain Power.* New York: Dodd, Mead and Co., 1985.

Gardner, Howard. *Frames of Mind: The Theory of Multiple Intelligences.* New York: Basic Books, 1983.

Gazzaniga, Michael S. *Nature's Mind.* New York: Harper Collins, 1992.

Goertzel, Victor, and Mildred George Goertzel. *Cradles of Eminence.* Boston: Little, Brown and Co., 1962.

Hutchison, Michael. *Mega Brain.* New York: Ballantine Books, 1991.

Le Poncin, Monique. *Brain Fitness.* New York: Fawcett Columbine, 1990.

Litvak, Stuart B. *Use Your Head.* Englewood Cliffs, NJ: Prentice-Hall, 1982.

Ornstein, Robert, and Richard F. Thompson. *The Amazing Brain.* Boston: Houghton-Mifflin, 1984.
— *The Evolution of Consciousness: Origins of the Way We Think.* New York: Simon and Schuster, 1991.

Restak, Richard, M.D. *The Brain.* New York: Bantam Books, 1984.
— *The Brain Has a Mind of Its Own.* New York: Harmony Books, 1991.
— *The Brain: The Last Frontier.* New York: Warner Books, 1979.

Silverstein, Alvin, and Virginia Silverstein. *World of the Brain.* New York: William Morrow and Co., 1986.

vos Savant, Marilyn. *Brain Building.* New York: Bantam Books, 1990.

Yepsen, Roger B. *How to Boost Your Brain Power.* Emmaus, PA: Rodale Press, 1987.
— *Smarten Up!* Boston: Little, Brown and Co., 1990.

The Brain video series (all 8 videos, $215; individually, $29.95). Available from: Annenberg CPB Project, PO Box 2345, South Burlington, VT 05407-2335; toll-free telephone 1-800-532-7637. A textbook and instructor's manual are available to accompany the series.

"Anamods"—two-dimensional cardboard cut-outs of brain sections which can be fitted together ($9.00)—are available from Damon Instructional Systems, 80 Wilson Way, Westward, MA 02090; toll-free telephone (800) 348-0025.

Human Half-Brain Models are available from Carolina Supply Company, 2700 York Road, Burlington, NC 27215. Right brain, cast from autopsy specimen, is about $65.00; left brain with detailed sculpturing is about $35.00. Both come with manuals.

Plastic Anatomical Models are available from Ideal School Supply Company, 11000 South Lavergne Avenue, Oak Lawn, IL 60453; telephone (708) 425-0800. "Human Brain with Skull" ($50.00) includes four removable sections; "Unassembled Brain Skull" can be painted ($14.00).

"The Nervous System" software (Apple II, 48K TRS-80, Model III) is available from Carolina Supply Company, 2700 York Road, Burlington, NC 27215 ($30.00).

Software on brain behavior is available at no cost from The Epilepsy Foundation, 4351 Garden City Drive, Landover, MD 20785; telephone (301) 459-3700.

Left-Brain and Right-Brain Thinking

Edwards, Betty. *Drawing On the Right Side of the Brain: A Course in Enhancing Creativity and Artistic Confidence.* Los Angeles: Jeremy P. Tarcher, Inc., 1989.

Ornstein, Robert. *The Psychology of Consciousness.* San Francisco, CA: W.H. Freeman and Co., 1972.

Springer, Sally P., and Georg Deutsch. *Left Brain, Right Brain.* San Francisco, CA: W.H. Freeman and Co., 1981.

Williams, Linda Verlee. *Teaching for the Two-Sided Mind.* Englewood Cliffs, NJ.: Prentice-Hall, 1983.

Zdenek, Marilee. *The Right Brain Experience.* New York: McGraw-Hill, 1983.

Problem-Solving, Creativity, and Thinking

Adams, James. *Conceptual Blockbusting.* New York: W.W. Norton and Co., 1979.

Burns, Marilyn. *The Book of Think or How to Solve a Problem Twice Your Size.* Boston: Little, Brown and Co., 1976.

De Bono, Edward. *Lateral Thinking: Creativity Step by Step.* New York: Harper and Row, 1970.

Eberle, Bob, and Bob Stanish. *CPS for Kids.* Buffalo, NY: D.O.K. Publishers, 1980.

Gordon, William J.J., and Tony Poze. *The New Art of the Possible.* Cambridge, MA: Porpoise Books, 1976.

Gourley, Theodore, and Samuel Micklus. *Problems, Problems, Problems!* Glassboro, NJ: Creative Competitions, 1982.

Koberg, Don, and Jim Bagnall. *The All New Universal Traveler.* Los Altos, CA: William Kaufman, Inc., 1981.

May, Rollo. *The Courage to Create.* New York: Bantam Books, 1975.

Raudsepp, Eugene. *Creative Growth Games.* New York: Perigee Books, 1977.

Stanish, Bob. *Mindanderings.* Carthage, IL: Good Apple, 1990.
— *The Ambidextrous Mind Book.* Carthage, IL: Good Apple, 1990.

Treffinger, Donald. *Encouraging Creative Learning for the Gifted and Talented.* Ventura, CA: Ventura County Superintendent of Schools Office, 1980.

von Oech, Roger. *A Kick in the Seat of the Pants.* New York: Harper and Row, 1986.
— *A Whack On the Side of the Head : How To Unlock Your Mind for Innovation.* New York: Warner Books, 1983.

Wonder, Jacquelyn and Donovan, Priscilla. *Whole Brain Thinking.* New York: William Morrow, 1984.

Imagination and Visual Thinking

Bagley, Michael, and Karin K. Hess. *200 Ways to Use Guided Imagery in the Classroom.* Unionville, NY: Trillium Press, 1984.

Hendricks, Gay, and Thomas B. Roberts. *The Second Centering Book: More Awareness Activities for Children, Parents and Teachers.* Englewood Cliffs, NJ: Prentice-Hall, 1977.

Eberle, Robert F. *SCAMPER: Games for Imagination Development.* Buffalo, NY: D.O.K. Publishers, 1977.
— *Visual Thinking.* Buffalo, NY: D.O.K. Publishers, 1981.

McKim, R. H. *Experiences in Visual Thinking.* Boston: PWS Engineering, 1980.

Walberg, Franette. *Puzzle Thinking.* Philadelphia: The Franklin Institute Press, 1980.

Inventing

Caney, Steven. *The Invention Book.* New York: Workman Publishing, 1985.

Flack, Jerry D. *Inventions and Inventors.* Englewood, CO: Teacher Ideas Press, 1989.

Keller, Charles. *The Best of Rube Goldberg, Inc.* Englewood Cliffs, NJ: Prentice-Hall, 1979.

Macauley, David. *The Way Things Work.* Boston: Houghton-Mifflin, 1988.

Muncy, Patricia Tyler. *Springboard to Creative Thinking: 101 Ready-to-Use Activities for Grades 3-8.* West Nyack, NY: Center for Applied Research in Education, 1988.

Murphy, Jim. *Weird and Wacky Inventions.* New York: Crown Publishers, 1978.

Scherr, George H. *The Journal of Irreproducible Results: Improbable Investigations and Unfounded Findings.* New York: Workman Publishing Co., 1983.

Stanish, Bob. *Inventioneering.* Carthage, IL: Good Apple, 1987.
— *Unconventional Invention Book.* Carthage, IL: Good Apple, 1981.

Memory and Learning

Brown, Alan S., Ph.D. *How to Increase Your Memory Power.* Glenview, IL: Scott, Foresman and Co., 1989.

Buzan, Tony. *Use Your Perfect Memory.* New York: E.P. Dutton, 1984.

Higbee, Kenneth L., Ph.D. *Your Memory: How It Works and How to Improve It.* New York: Paragon House, 1993.

Lorayne, Harry. *How to Develop a Super Power Memory.* Hollywood, FLA: 1989.

Montgomery, Robert L. *Memory Made Easy.* New York: Amacom Publishing, 1979.

Sandstrom, Robert. *The Ultimate Memory Book.* Granada Hills, CA: Stepping Stone Books, 1990.

TLC for Your Brain

Maguire, Jac. *Care and Feeding of the Brain.* New York: Doubleday, 1990.

Thinking Challenges

Block, J.R., and Harold E. Yuker. *Can You Believe Your Eyes?* New York: Gardner Press, 1984.

Gardner, Robert. *Experimenting with Illusions.* New York: Franklin Watts, 1990.

Gudeman, Janice. *Creative Encounters With Creative People.* Carthage, IL: Good Apple, 1984.

Shushan, Ronnie, ed. *GAMES Big Book of Games.* New York: Workman Publishing, 1984.

Winter, Arthur, M.D., and Ruth. *Build Your Brain Power.* New York: St. Martin's Press, 1986.

CHALLENGE Magazine. Good Apple Publications, 1204 Buchanan St., Box 299, Carthage, IL 62321; telephone (217) 357-3981.

OMNI Magazine. OMNI Publications International LTD, 1965 Broadway, New York, N.Y. 10023; toll-free telephone 1-800-289-6664.

INDEX

Other Great Books from Free Spirit

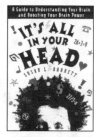

It's All in Your Head
A Guide to Understanding Your Brain and Boosting Your Brain Power
by Susan L. Barrett
This updated "owner's manual" on the brain includes new brain facts; new definitions of intelligence and creativity; new facts on how diet, exercise, and sleep affect the brain; and more. For ages 9–14.
$9.95; 160 pp.; softcover; illus.; 6" x 9"

Making the Most of Today
Daily Readings for Young People on Self-Awareness, Creativity, and Self-Esteem
by Pamela Espeland and Rosemary Wallner
Quotes from famous figures guide you through a year of positive thinking, problem solving, and practical lifeskills—the keys to making the most of every day. For ages 11 & up.
$9.95; 392 pp.; softcover; 4¼" x 6¼"

School Power
Strategies for Succeeding in School
by Jeanne Shay Schumm, Ph.D., and Marguerite C. Radencich, Ph.D.
Covers getting organized, taking notes, studying smarter, following directions, handling homework, managing long-term assignments, and more.
For ages 11 & up.
$13.95; 132 pp.; softcover; B&W photos & illus.; 8½" x 11"

Psychology for Kids
40 Fun Tests That Can Help You Learn About Yourself
by Jonni Kincher
Based on sound psychological concepts, these fascinating tests promote self-discovery, self awareness, and self-esteem and empower young people to make good choices.
For ages 10 & up.
$14.95; 152 pp.; softcover; illus.; 8½" x 11"

The Kid's Guide to Social Action
How to Solve the Social Problems You Choose—and Turn Creative Thinking into Positive Action
Revised, Updated, and Expanded Edition
by Barbara A. Lewis
A comprehensive guide to making a difference in the world. Teaches letter writing, interviewing, speechmaking, fundraising, lobbying, getting media coverage, and more.
For ages 10 & up.
$16.95; 232 pp.; softcover; B&W photos & illus.; 8½" x 11"

Challenging Projects for Creative Minds
12 Self-Directed Enrichment Projects That Develop and Showcase Student Ability for Grades 1–5
by Phil Schlemmer, M.Ed., and Dori Schlemmer
The best way to prepare children for the future is to teach them how to learn, and that's just what these projects do. Each project sparks kids' imaginations, calls on their creativity, and challenges them to solve problems, find and use information, and think for themselves. For teachers, grades 1–5.
$29.95; 120 pp.; softcover; illus.; 8½" x 11"

Stick Up for Yourself!
Every Kid's Guide to Personal Power and Positive Self-Esteem
by Gershen Kaufman, Ph.D., and Lev Raphael, Ph.D.
Simple text teaches assertiveness, responsibility, relationship skills, choice making, problem solving, and goal setting. For ages 8–12.
$9.95; 96 pp.; softcover; illus.; 6" x 9"

Teacher's Guide
by Gerri Johnson, Gershen Kaufman, Ph.D., and Lev Raphael, Ph.D.
For teachers, grades 3–7.
$18.95; 128 pp.; softcover; 8½" x 11"

Challenging Projects for Creative Minds
20 Self-Directed Enrichment Projects That Develop and Showcase Student Ability for Grades 6 & Up
by Phil Schlemmer, M.Ed., and Dori Schlemmer
Give your students opportunities to explore beyond core curriculum by completing in-depth projects that promote lifelong learning skills. Reproducible forms help students choose and plan a project, report their progress and problems, keep record of their work time, and evaluate the project after completion. For teachers, grades 6 & up.
$34.95; 148 pp.; softcover; illus.; 8½" x 11"

To place an order or to request a free catalog of SELF–HELP FOR KIDS® materials, please write, call, email, or visit our Web site:

Free Spirit Publishing Inc.
400 First Avenue North • Suite 616 • Minneapolis, MN 55401-1724
toll-free 800.735.7323 • local 612.338.2068 • fax 612.337.5050
help4kids@freespirit.com • www.freespirit.com